# Easy Writer

*10 Steps to Writing a Best Selling Book that Wows Your Readers and Turns them into Paying Clients*

This book was written by Vickie Gould, Law of Attraction Business and Book Coach. www.vickiegould.com email vickie@vickiegould.com

# Acknowledgement

Thank you to the 92 authors who have taught me during the process of writing and publishing their best sellers. It is your experiences that have helped me know what to put inside this book.

To all the future authors reading this, I commend your courage to share your stories so that they can create positive change and impact lives around the world. It is because of the calling on your life to write your book that we can make a difference, share inspiration and give hope.

# Table of Contents

Don't forget to download your

## free workbook companion

at **bit.ly/EWWorkbook**

AND

## 5 Secret Strategies to
## Write Your Book Quickly

at **bit.ly/5secretstrategies**

# Want to listen to Easy Writer?

## Get the audiobook for just $7.00 here:

http://bit.ly/easywriteraudiobook

# Preface

Some people know me as The Words Lady™ and if I was interviewed on the radio, they would open up with the fact that I've helped nearly 100 entrepreneurs get the story out of their belly and become best selling authors. I help them create a revenue stream based on their story and what they do with their story. My authors have been on Tedx, TV, and radio and have had book signings across the world. They've closed $2M deals after their success as an author and reached hundreds of people internationally with their message.

But what you might not know is there was a time where I thought I could outrun my own story.

It was back in early 1989. It was the second semester of my senior year of high school and another potentially horrid night with my mother. My dad wasn't home which meant my buffer was gone.

Now my mom stood five foot four inches but when she screamed I could swear she was 6'9". Though she weighed probably 100 pounds, somehow she seemed like she had the muscles and the strength, when she was angry with me, of a body builder 4 times my size.

Don't get me wrong -- I love my mother. But for some reason I reminded my mother of all of her greatest failures. For some reason I reminded my mother of everything she couldn't do or have. I don't know whether it was because I had her eyes. I don't know whether it was because I have her fiery personality, but all I know was that night she had me in a headlock. And every now and again, I boldly put her in one too.

She yanked my hair and I yanked hers back

and she grabbed my arm so hard it left a handprint shaped bruise. I got away and I ran up the stairs and I said, "I'm done. I'm done. I'm so done."

I furiously packed my things and like a studious Asian, I packed my school books because of course I would be going to school the next day and my contact lens solution. I failed to pack my underwear!

For some reason I found a bungee cord in my closet. I hooked it to one leg of my canopy. I tied my sheets to it. Then strung it out the window. And just so you know – it's not like the movies where when you gracefully go down the side of a building like boing boing boing boing boing. With a bungee cord you just land -- DOINK.

But don't worry. I was OK. I saw the light of a gas station in the distance and somehow I ran there. I don't remember how I even got there.

I used the pay phone to call a friend to pick me up and I vowed I would never go back.

But the words kept going through my head –it was that story I thought I was outrunning. It replayed over and over.

You're not going to amount to anything.

You're worthless.

Lay down on the floor and die.

I wish I never had you.

You're not enough.

Once I became successful I actually didn't want to tell anyone that story. In my culture, it would shame the family name.  But since then, amidst all tears and confusion of the "Why did I have to go through that?" I realized that you can turn your pain and your mess into your message when you can bring value and purpose to the things you've gone through … you can become the wounded changemaker and I became committed to helping others do just that. You can become the way shower. See, I first had to learn how to embrace my story.  Then I could teach others how to make a best seller out of theirs.

Grab the Easy Writer workbook companion here: https://vickiegould.com/easy-writer-workbook-download/ (bit.ly/EWWorkbook)

# Introduction:

# Who Are You to Write a Book?

*Twenty years from now you will be more disappointed by the things that you didn't do than by the ones you did do.*
*- H.Jackson Brown Jr., P.S. I Love You*

Growing up in an Asian household, education and music were a huge part of life. If my sister and I weren't studying, we were playing the piano. Most everything else was considered a waste of time. Now don't feel sorry for me, I did go outside to play sometimes, but most of the time I stayed indoors.

In order to avoid getting in trouble or being assigned extra piano time, I kept my nose in fiction books from the library. Every week I went to the public library, checked out the maximum of 10 books and hastily returned home to read. My favorite place to read was sitting sideways in the yellow velvet living room armchair by the front window. Right outside the window, past the porch was a pink cherry blossom tree that I would gaze out at while I imagined the characters in the books I was reading.

After a while, I read the whole entire library. From "Are You There God? It's Me, Margaret" to "Anne Frank's Diary" to "Little Women" and "Around the World in 80 Days," I enjoyed being able to see the world and go on adventures without ever leaving the comfort of that armchair.

From that time, I dreamt that I would one day be an author. It seemed so glamorous, fun and exciting. As I married and had kids, I imagined being the grandma in a rocking chair telling stories that the grandkids would hang on. Whenever I read a story to my children, it was always with gusto, different voices per character and pauses for emphasis. One of my boys likes the theatrical nature of my reading better than the other.

As my 40's came, I was still thinking about writing that book "one day." Then 45 came and it still wasn't done. I thought, "Who am I to write this book?" and "I don't even know what I should write about."

Those thoughts were followed by, "No one is going to want to read your book," and "You're not that interesting." I wondered if I wrote it who would want to read it and if it would be at all useful. In my younger years, I had wanted to write fiction but as I got older, I wanted to write about my own experiences and share knowledge.

My first book was about my journey with

chronic Lyme Disease where I shared the struggles and some of the protocols I tried. It wasn't directed only towards Lyme Disease sufferers – it was for those with chronic illness. As I went to publish it, rather than be afraid of who wouldn't read it, I was scared that someone actually would read it! What if I got judged? What if they hated it? And even though I hit the publish button on Amazon, I barely told anyone it was available because I was afraid it wasn't up to par.

Now that I've published and released 9 best selling books and helped 92 others become best sellers too, I've since overcome those fears. I'll tell you more about how you can overcome these same exact thoughts that went through my head and those of my clients as you read this book so that you can feel the full joy of become a published (and even best selling) author.

I'll be sharing some of my past client

experiences in the "Coaching Chronicles" section of this book. Their names have been changed.

It's simple to give you steps to sharing your story or structuring your book, but it's your confidence that will help you most to hit publish. This is why I wrote this book – so that you not only know how to write the book but you also release it so it can help others, leave your legacy and create more impact in your life and business. The more people you can help, the more good you can do in this world.

Besides, I know as well as you probably do too, that if you've been called to write a book, that calling will not go away until it's done. Answer the nudge.

You can do this!

# Step 1:

# Decide What Kind of Author You Are

*Ask for what you want*
*and be prepared to get it.*
*- Maya Angelou*

If you've picked up this book, I'm guessing you have a business -- you're an entrepreneur who wants to attract more prospects and have more sales. A book can definitely help you do that if you use it properly but you have to decide how you're going to use it from the beginning so you can reverse engineer your own success.

The sad truth about book writing is that most authors only sell about 250 copies of their book over the life of the book. If you want to make your time writing your book worthwhile to your business, you have to connect that book with your main selling product. It must be aligned and flow right into your product if it is going to work to help turn prospects into paying clients.

Now if you want to write a book just to say you did it, you want it for vanity's sake, that's perfectly fine. I will never try to make someone wrong for that. However, that's not the focus of this book. We are talking about writing non-fiction books that will grow your business and income.

Writing a book can help to create the freedom you want in your business and life. I know it's easy to want the book and blame time for why you haven't written it yet. As my husband often says, "You make time for what's important."

In the fall of 1995, while I was pregnant with my first child, I accepted a new job at Comerica Bank. I was 26 years old, an Assistant Vice President in the risk department, married and a homeowner. By all looks, life was perfect. I had a corner office cubicle with windows and drove a dark blue Infiniti QX4.

I had followed my mother's teachings to get a good education at the University of Michigan and get a corporate job. In the last five years since graduation, I had changed jobs about every two years, getting a nice increase in pay. Climb the corporate ladder and the happiness pot of gold would be at the end, or so I thought.

When my daughter was born on June 5th, I lamented the day I had to put her into day care over the summer. I wanted to snuggle with her little face all day long, kiss her pudgy cheeks and smell her sweet baby head. It had only been six weeks since her birth and I was pumping breast milk to pack for her care.

Two weeks later she came down with bronchitis for the first time. I knew she caught it from day care, but I couldn't do anything about it, I had to go back to work. So after a day on antibiotics, I reluctantly sent her back. She was okay for a few weeks and then she caught bronchitis again.

This cycle of on and off again bronchitis went on through the fall and winter. I wasn't getting any sleep because I was rocking her in the dim of her nightlight, keeping her upright so she could breathe through her clogged up tiny little nose. That cushioned glider rocking chair became my bed for the next 6 months.

By late March I called my sister, "I can't do this anymore," I sobbed. "I'm exhausted. I can't keep sending her back."

It was then I decided that I needed to find another job that wasn't so demanding where I could be with her more and not have to send her to daycare.

At first I thought the solution was to get a commissioned job like stockbroker, realtor or mortgage executive. I tried all three and it became quite evident that although I did have a more flexibility with my schedule, I still had to report to someone and couldn't call my own shots. I couldn't take vacations whenever I wanted and by then I had three kids. I was taking sales calls from my car, telling the kids to shush.

Now I didn't go directly into becoming an entrepreneur after that, but I always had entrepreneurial side gigs like soap making, card stamping, cake decorating, crafting lotions and herbal concoctions, making jewelry and the like but I never had the nerve to strike out entirely on my own until I looked into becoming a coach.

Coaching came naturally to me because of my empathic and intuitive nature and that still serves me well. Additionally, the possibilities for success in whatever way you want to define it are limitless. You get to create whatever business fits your lifestyle.

Because of my past corporate jobs in statistics and finance, I knew that I wanted a business that could work without me. As a stockbroker, we called that annuitizing your business where you could walk away for a while and know that you were still going to be paid. I knew I needed a way to do that -- I wanted automation and a funnel (even before I knew what a funnel was). And it wasn't right away, but I soon realized that a book was an integral part of my business strategy because it would help me do just that.

Most people don't write the book because they don't see what they're losing from not having it done. I'm going to assume you would love to have 3 extra clients per month or more. Maybe that would help you hit 5-figure months or more but instead, you're slaving away at being in Facebook groups, trying to get over 10k followers on Instagram, or looking for the perfect connections on Linkedin.

What if you could get your finished book into the hands of 10 potential ideal clients per month. What is your closing rate? 20-30 percent? Could you turn those people who have read your book which is highly aligned with your business vision, purpose and product into an upsold reader who eagerly buys your product? If you could gain 2 to 3 extra clients from those 10 people, how would that change your life? THAT is what you're missing out on, my friend, without your book.

At this moment it may still feel overwhelming, but by the end of this book, it shouldn't. I've been told over and over again that one of the things people appreciate about me is that I can take something that feels hard or complicated and turn it into easy to understand steps. I'm going to do that for you too.

*The following is an article that I originally wrote for Writer's Digest:*

I'm getting that deer-in-the-headlights look as a response again.

When people tell me they want to write a book and they need help, I always ask, "What's the purpose of your book?"

All too often I get that look along with, "I haven't really thought about that," or "I just want to inspire people." Usually they're more concerned about asking me which topic I think they should write on or if I think their storyline is good, but you can't pick either until you know the answer to the above question because you won't know why you're even writing.

Is the book supposed to be a great story? Entertainment? To steal away to fantasy-land? Or is it to grow your business? To teach something important? To share your journey to entrepreneurial success?

What do you want the reader to get out of the reading experience? And what is your goal for writing the book?

According to Pollster, over 80 percent of Americans want to write a book. Maybe it's purely to check off, "wrote a book" from the bucket list. Sometimes it's because there's something important to teach, like a seven-step process. Other times, it's to write a novel, poetry or memoir.

If you want to write a book, for whatever

reason, it's important to know what kind of author you actually want to be so you know what strategy to use to sell books.

**Author-Author vs. Author-Entrepreneur**

You see, there are two types of authors. I like to call them, "author-authors" and "author-entrepreneurs." The main difference between the two is that author-entrepreneurs own a business that their book is tied to and they make a living off of their business, which is partially fed by their book.

Let's take a look at the two profiles.

Author-authors:

- Have books as their only product
- Create income solely from book sales and royalties
- Their business is books
- May write fiction or non-fiction

- Call themselves an "author" as their primary title

Author-entrepreneurs:

- Have a business that is tied to the subject of the book
- They use their book as leverage to feed sales of their other products or services
- Don't care very much about royalties and may give books away
- Create income mainly from sales of products outside of their books
- Generally write non-fiction
- Call themselves by their business title and "author" secondarily

## How Marketing Strategies Differ by Goal

You need to know which one you are because it dictates how you run your business, and yes, both are businesses. If you are an author-author, then you will focus on book sales, period.

If you are an author-entrepreneur, you will focus on leveraging your book to get bigger sales on your other products. You are in the business of turning readers into clients. Your book is a marketing tool, not your bread and butter.

Author-authors also generally have higher goals for the number of books they want to sell each month. That's not to say that author-entrepreneurs don't have big goals too, but they have the potential to reach their income goals with fewer book sales.

For example, if you leverage your book and seed it properly inside, allowing you to upsell your reader into your $500 product or $3,000 coaching package, how many books would you need to sell to hit your monthly income goal? Compare that to royalty checks and you'll see that it would take far more from book sales alone to hit the same goal.

Neither type of author is better or worse; it just depends on what you want from your writing. Both have the potential of being a great way to make your living.

Here's the thing though, you have to choose which one you want to be. You can't have one foot in each camp or else your focus becomes cloudy.

How would it be if one day you want to sell your book for the maximum price because you're acting like an author-author and the next day, you're giving it away to a potential upsell client thinking they're worth a free book because you might get a sale in the hundreds or thousands range. This just won't do!

So you have to choose and now is the moment of truth. Which type of author do you want to be?

I hope you don't have that deer-in-the-headlights look. (1)

## Coaching Chronicles

"I just want to share my story to inspire people. I know that people can relate to what I went through and I want people to know that if a poor little girl with a learning disability from the inner city who grew up in an abusive household can rise above, they can do it too," Kristal said to me. "If I can help just one person it will be worth it."

Lies!

While it's true that if your book helps just one person, it's worth it, no one really aspires to write a book to have just one person be changed. We want to help that one person AND help millions because it's completely possible. It's an "and" type of thing. It's okay to say so too.

Is it really true that you'd be okay with affecting just one person in this world? If not, own that you want more and write your book to that end.

How can you create the most impact and change in the world? By enrolling people into your products and services from your book. The more people that you can help at a deeper level than just your book, the bigger your waves of change will be.

While it may seem tempting to always sell your book in the beginning because 10 bucks for your book sounds good, if that $10 book could bring you a $1000 client if you gave it away for free, would you? Even if you had to give away 10 books to get that one client, would it still be worth it?

Always see the bigger picture. Keep the end

goal in mind – the upsell of your bigger product.

## Summary

Some authors write because they want to live off book royalties. Their business is their book.

Others write because it will help make it easier to gain more clients in another business.

There's a difference between an author who writes for book profits and one who writes to upsell the reader.  Which do you want to be?

Grab the Easy Writer workbook companion here: https://vickiegould.com/easy-writer-workbook-download/ (bit.ly/EWWorkbook)

# Step 2:

# What You Need to Have in Place to Profit from Your Book

*You have brains in your head.*
*You have feet in your shoes. You can steer*
*yourself any direction you choose.*
*-Dr. Seuss*

When I was a health coach I felt guilty for asking to be paid for my expertise in chronic illness, detox and Lyme Disease. It seemed selfish to ask those potentially on disability to pay me for my time.

Coming from a heart-centered mission for my business, I felt guilty almost every day so I gave everything away for free. People could message me and get on the phone with me for free advice and personalized plans for healing. In some ways, all the hours I gave away made me feel great, in other ways, it just made me feel overworked and underpaid... and underappreciated.

When I wrote my first best seller, "No Energy, No Life, No Problem," I gave that away too. Even though I had a program they could join after people read the book, I didn't really mention it. So while I had a best seller, I had zero profits, no business growth and no impact. I had no plan.

Many people come to me after they've written their book asking how they can monetize it. Problem is, they didn't ask before they wrote their book.

The result is a book that may be disjoint from their current business which means that book won't do much to create profits for the business. It may also create confusion with readers because they won't see the correlation between the book and what you do, and a confused buyer doesn't buy.

Putting out a book that is misaligned with your business can actually be a detriment to your profits as it could repel your potential client too.

So you must be able to answer the question, "What action do you want the reader to take once they're done reading your book?" If you don't know, you might be writing your book too soon.

But don't worry, you can fix the "too soon" syndrome pretty quickly by having a few things in place before you write it so that you know you have the potential to reap big returns on investment from writing your book. In face, I did a YouTube video about this very thing. Take a listen to the video:

https://youtu.be/CHw7gH2pFlQ

Imagine what your life could look like if you had your mission, purpose, message, story and Best Selling book all aligned with your signature coaching packages and products and could automate a system that would get you appointments on autopilot with readers who are eager to become clients.

First, as I say a lot, start with the end in mind. Again, what is it that you want your reader to take action on by the time they're done reading (or even before they're finished)? Most will respond with, "Buy my product/coaching package/service." Remember this is where all the profit it made.

You need five critical pieces in place to maximize your profits.

## 1. A Clear message
Your prospect needs to know exactly what

you're about if they're going to buy your book (or exchange their email for a free copy).

What's the main thing you want them to think when they see you? What do you want them to associate with you? For example, I want people to associate "The Words Lady™," book coach, and law of attraction practitioner when they think of me. I want it to be a knee-jerk reaction.

## 2. A Signature Package/Product

What's that thing that you want people to upsell into? It's also another association like above. For me, it's Easy Writer (the book you're reading), Easy Writer Guaranteed Amazon Best Seller Program (my signature group program) and Impact (my private 1:1 coaching package).

Please don't be overwhelmed by this. If you don't have a program or product yet, it's easy to offer something like a three month private 1:1 coaching package.

## 3. An Enticing Freebie

I'm sure you've heard it before – the money is in your list so growing your list should be a top priority. And because Amazon will never release email addresses of your purchasers, you have to find a different way to gather those emails.

Your freebie should be enticing to your reader and match up with your book. Think of what else they would need from you. What would someone need before they need you? What could be an overview to share?

Templates and checklists work well. Webinar and challenges are harder to get people into because they have to commit more time.

## 4. Your Finished Best Selling Book

I know it probably goes without saying, but if you want to profit from your book, you have to finish writing it! If you look at most of the gurus out there, they have books. Why? Because they work! Some of them have been using the same book for many years and that same book continues to annually grow their business and create more clients (and more income) consistently.

This is a perfect example of why you must have your book aligned with what you want your reader to buy. Do that well and you might have a one and done book, although most of my best selling authors tell me it was such an enjoyable process and so fulfilling that they want to write another book – this from people who initially said they wanted to just write one book!

## 5. A Complete Book Funnel

A funnel is a description of a prospect's journey from hearing about you to purchasing your product or service. If you haven't heard of a funnel before, it's a must-have in profiting from your book.

Stages of a Funnel

Awareness – your prospect finds out about you and your expertise

Interest – your prospect is increasing in curiosity on how you can help them

Desire – your prospect is growing in their want. They may be aspiring to be more like you.

Action – taking the next step towards purchasing your product or service

When creating your book funnel, you may start with a freebie, entice them to purchase your book, send them an email nurture sequence and then upsell them into your signature product or service.

That last piece, the upsell, is where your profit is.

Coaching Chronicles

"Can I skip some of these things?" asked Doris. She was cringing as I shared the pieces she needed to fully profit from the time she was going to spend writing her book. "What if I did all that for my next book instead?"

My response as her coach was to say I can't force her to do anything. Everyone has their free choice, but what I do know after helping nearly 100 others become best sellers is that those who have these pieces in place are better equipped to sell their product or service multiple times over.

Sure it's fun to go speak at an event and have a book signing table in the back. Sure it's fun to sell books and have people tell you how much they liked it. But wouldn't it be more fun if those same people became bigger clients where you could have a bigger impact in their lives because they had access to your other programs?

This goes back to chapter one. Are you an author-author or an author-entrepreneur?

And if you're tempted to skip the book funnel, think of the last time you wanted something and were told it wasn't available. You have an awareness, an interest and a desire. How did you feel when you couldn't take action? That's how you'll leave your prospect (your reader).

Summary

There are critical pieces to your business to have in place if you want to fully benefit from writing your best seller.

For each thing you skip, you risk lowering your profit potential.

1. A Clear Message

2. A Signature Package/Product

3. An Enticing Freebie

4. Your Finished Best Selling Book

5. Complete book funnel

Need help putting these items together? Check out my 60 Day Biz Bookcamp at https://member.vickiegould.com/60-day-biz-bookcamp-home/ (bit.ly/60daybizbookcamp)
Use code :EASYWRITERBOOK for $100 off

Grab the Easy Writer workbook companion here: https://vickiegould.com/easy-writer-workbook-download/ (bit.ly/EWWorkbook)

# Step 3:

# Decide to Hide or Shine

*I have learned over the years that when one's*
*mind is made up, this diminishes fear.*
*-Rosa Parks*

Are you ready to bunk the statistics? Over
80% of the population wants to write a book,
but 97% of them never finish. Then, out of the
3% left, only 20% of them actually publish
their book. That means that for every 1000
people who want to write a book, 30 people
finish and only 6 hit publish -- that's .6
percent. Yikes!

Before you even start to write your book, you
have to decide if you're going to stay silent
and hide or if you're willing to potentially be
uncomfortable and shout about your book

from the rooftops because without visibility you'll have zero impact. That one person you said you'd be happy to help won't even be able to find you, let alone impact thousands or millions of people around the world.

If you don't want your book to just be a check box off your list of things you want to do then you have to be ready and willing to share your genius with the world.

Guess what? People might stare. People might judge. People might not like you. Someone might hate your book. And the horror -- someone might disagree with you!

In fact, it's happened to me twice now out of the 9 best sellers I've published. It felt like a stab in the heart and I questioned whether it was a good idea for me to even continue to write. I questioned if I could be a good book coach with a bad review. I wondered if I would lose potential clients if they saw those reviews. I was horrified that I'd be laughed at.

When I realized that it was more about helping others than it was about my comfort level, I became more bold about my message and less concerned about who I might "offend" because they didn't agree with me or my methods (or plain didn't like my style of writing).

Many of my clients have also wondered what people will think if they know _____ about them.  I'll be judged.  Worse yet, I'll be shunned, made fun of -- I don't want to tell my story and then feel like it's a mistake.

Yet I don't know anyone who has shared heir story that hasn't gotten such rave feedback, people coming up to them saying that they're so happy they shared because the same or similar happened to them and they really needed to hear it. They needed to know they were not alone and that someone understood.

That's usually what the reaction is.

I want you to close your eyes and visualize a large crowd or auditorium filled with people.

Imagine these are all the people that have been touched and changed by your story because you had the courage to share it. What do you see in their lives that have changed?  Pick one out of the crowd.  What would they say to you?

Imagine someone saying to you, "I was at the end of my rope. I didn't know how I'd get through. I didn't know what to do next or where to turn. Then I heard your story and it inspired to me to change my life in the area of (fill in your specialty).  My life has never been the same.  I see such positivity all around me. I've been able to accomplish _____.
Thank you for sharing.  It was exactly what I needed at the right time."

Now feel the disappointment of not sharing your story --- that auditorium is now empty. There are random people in the world you were supposed to touch that walk around with sad faces and depression. They struggle – I want you to really feel that because most of the time we don't take action because we don't feel the disappointment now.

Just like many don't worry about the consequences of smoking or drinking too much so that we stop doing something or start doing something like eating healthier, getting more sleep, or lowering stress because there is no consequence today, at this very moment. We aren't feeling the pain.

How does that hit you?

Listen, when you make your story, your book and your life not about you and your fears, but more about how you can help others and create change and impact the world, it's easier to get over your fears (notice I didn't say your fears won't exist). Many times I push aside fears for the bigger thing I'm going to experience (and others will experience) because that matters more.

Of course you'll have those scared feelings the first time you do something – it's similar to that big rollercoaster you want to try but you are scared. You have all that heart-pounding anticipation waiting in line, looking up to see how tall it is and then you do it. It's so much fun that you want to do it again. The reward for facing that scared feeling is the fun and excitement just like that.

The change we make in others lives is like the fun we get to experience on that rollercoaster too.

Coaching Chronicles

Sarah came to me with an idea for a series of

books. The titles would be the same but the subtitles would share a different angle. While the topics were enticing, the problem was that she didn't have many followers on social media.

We knew that without interest, she wouldn't sell any books and it would jeopardize her chances to hit best seller. She needed a community.

So we came up with a plan to use quotes from her book, ask people for input on what they'd want to hear and videos sharing the progress she was making writing the book.

A phenomenal thing started to happen. As she shared the book, her perspective, her stories and herself, people started to fall in love with her. They began to be invested in the book she was writing and in a couple months she had amassed thousands of followers!

The day she launched her book, she hit best seller before lunchtime!

How did she do it? She decided to shine. She chose to become visible even if it was new and sometimes uncomfortable. She knew that the people she wanted to serve deserved to hear about her book and it would be more painful for her to stay hidden.

<u>Summary</u>

It's not worth writing a book if you don't plan on mentioning it to anyone. It will sit on the shelf collecting dust and it will end up being just a checkmark in your life of something you did. If you truly believe that your story will help someone in the world, you must choose to be bold.

If you hide, you can't make the impact you want, so decide before you start writing how you're going to show up.

Grab the Easy Writer workbook companion here: https://vickiegould.com/easy-writer-workbook-download/ (bit.ly/EWWorkbook)

# Why Me?

Many people have watched me travel around the world and wear cool high heel shoes at my events and speaking gigs, which symbolize my overcoming Lyme Disease. They see me as inspiring and positive, smiling and joking much of the time.

But what might be surprising to know is there was a helpless, sad time in my life where I seriously contemplated taking my own life.

Back in November of 2009, I was diagnosed with Chronic Lyme Disease and I remember the day that the doctor swung around on is little doctor's stool and he said to me, "You need to treat your body like it's an 80 year old body and you're not going to get it back."

And I thought, "Could this really be true? Is this what my life is destined to be like?" Was this going to be a long drawn out death for the next 40-50 years?  You see, Lyme has no set protocol and there's no cure.

So I went home and I called my sister and I asked her, if it takes me, you have to promise me to tell my children who I really was because I didn't think they would ever get to know me. I was spending 16-18 hours in bed every day.

Three and a half years passed this way - 1,176 days I spent sun up to sun down too exhausted and in pain to do anything.   My thoughts were my constant companion and they told me things like ... you're nothing, you're draining the family finances, no help is coming, no one wants you, you're going to die like this. Over and over again I heard those words in my head.

And as I watched my children grow up by the side of my bed, I felt the guilt of not volunteering anymore, not being at their sporting events and not being a good mom or wife.

When my youngest, Trenton, would climb into bed and snuggle up to me, I'd see the hopefulness in his eyes as he asked me if I could come to his school party and then the sadness wash over them as I told him that, "Mama just isn't up to it."

And I'd wonder, "Does he know how much I love him? Will he grow up to resent me? Will he ever know how much I really wanted to go? and will he ever understand how much it hurt my heart to tell him no?"

And the thing about it was, I desperately wanted it to end. I didn't want to hide at night anymore, crying in the bathroom, huddled on the cold little floor mat so that I wouldn't wake my husband up.

I just wanted the misery to end. But I didn't really want my life to end. I longingly wanted to be around to see my grandchildren and to be able to play with them. It just didn't seem possible at the time.

But something in me said that my children, my husband, my future grandchildren were worth fighting for. And I wanted to live my legacy today as I lived, rather than in my sister's words as I requested after I died.

So I began to not listen to what the doctor said about that 80 year old woman. I decided to believe more in myself than what that doctor was telling me. And I began to be at that time, the 42 year old woman that I was. Matter of fact, the 42 year old mother waiting for her children to grow up. I taught myself how to relieve my issues with herbs and alternative modalities and the good days started out number the bad.

And as I did that, I realized that so many people have risen above their pain. Have dug down into their tenacity and perseverance and they all have great stories as well. So I began to apply my own determination, along with my creativity and my ability to produce Best Selling authors and I began to invite people to write their story, show their story and share their story as I do today.

It's time for you too to show your story now. That moment in your life when you screamed out, "Why me?!" was exactly for this moment where you can share with another human that they're not alone, that they can do it, that there is someone in their corner.

What if that story inside of you was orchestrated for you to show up in someone's life and you never let it out? What struggle did you go through that you would've given anything to get out of? There are people waiting for you to show up in their lives. Don't let them wait too long.


Join us in the Write Your Biz Book Facebook Group for a community of other author-entrepreneurs, more coaching and free trainings here:

www.facebook.com/groups/vickiegouldcoaching

# Step 4:

# How to Write a Story that Captures Your Reader

*People will forget what you said, people will forget what you did, but people will never forget how you made them feel.*
*-Maya Angelou*

When I first started business coaching, I was a story marketing coach. I helped people to craft their stories to be magnetic to their audience because these days, people crave relationships. They want to be with and buy from people who are relatable and real. They want to know something more about you than just what you do. They want to know your why.

So let's talk about sharing your journey – you

know – that one that is unique to you, that was orchestrated just for you so that you could fulfill your purpose, passion and calling.

Sometimes we wonder why we've gone through tough times in life. Whether it's really impactful, pretty tragic, or just plain every day tough stuff, it's easy to think "Why me?" I know I did. I cried, I felt sorry for myself, I got angry at God, I was angry with myself but worst of all, I was bitter because of the regrets I had.

We were not meant to be tumbleweeds going through life without a purpose or reason. Your journey was only for you and meant to help you develop and grow into the YOU you needed to be in order to help the world.

Whether your world is your family, your community, your state, your nation or the entire world, people are waiting to hear from you so that they can get the help they need.

Your journey is important to them.  Your story matters and you need to share it!

Here's the other thing, people remember stories. Think about when you get excited or interested about something. Think about when you last got together with a friend.  What did you share?  Stories maybe?

*"There is no greater agony than bearing an untold story inside you." Maya Angelou*

The name of the game when you're writing a book is to get the reader to keep turning pages. You need to be compelling, engaging and magnetic. Your story needs some basic components if you want to intrigue that client and get them to buy from to you.

Wouldn't it be nice if you could put your story out there, people began to talk about you and your expertise, and then clients came to you rather than you chasing them down?  Do you think it's out of the realms of possibilities with you?  It can happen.  And it will happen if you share your story enough, in the right way.

There is a structure of a story that will catch the interest of your ideal client and remember it's not a timeline. A timeline is boring! Please do not start with, "I was born …. And then in elementary school …. .and then …. And then I got married … and then ….." What you are going to share in your story is a moment in your life. You must show, not tell (which is the name of my course on storytelling because it's that important).

Here are the critical four components to put in your story:

1. The call – this is when you get called into action.  Something spurned you to do something.  What was it?  This is where your audience relates to you and says – yes, that's me too.

2.  The Hole – here is where you enter the depths of darkness, wondering how to get out of it.  You want to convey emotions as vulnerable and raw as possible.

The more private your thoughts are, the more universal and connected it becomes.  I've had people tell me that they went through the exact same thing I did after hearing my story, but when they tell me their story, I only see bits and pieces of similarities.

What they're relating to is the emotion and feelings that I invoked in them.  For example, if you have a story that makes someone feel sadness, they'll think of a time they were sad over something and the something may not be even close to what your something is but the emotion is.

Emotions are where people buy from so it's important to be very real in this area. If you're going to spend any extra time in any of the four components, this is the place to share more.

If you're wondering how much to share, if you're wondering if you should "go there," the answer is YES! That place that you might be thinking is too much, that you think no one wants to hear, or that you might be tempted to gloss over is exactly what your reader wants to hear!

The hole is also the way to increase the speed of trust. When you take your turn to be vulnerable first, others feel safe to be vulnerable with you too. You'll automatically enter deeper conversations right away and convert clients faster.

This is where you can start getting excited about being uncomfortable. Being vulnerable here will likely cost you something. That's how you know your story is good.

3. The Journey – this is where you go looking for answers or the truth. While telling your story, we wonder if you're going to get out. This search creates anticipation. This is where they're sitting on the edge of their seats, mesmerized by what you're saying.

The steps that you took to get out of the hole in the journey are the steps in your program that people will want you to help them with.

4. The A-ha – this is where you breathe a sigh of relief because you found the solution, the answer, or arrived at the end of the tunnel. Your a-ha moment makes you an expert. This establishes your credibility. Do this right and people will rarely ask you for your credentials. Life has taught you all you need to know.

Because you've connected your vulnerability to this a-ha, you won't have to convince someone in other ways that you are capable or have the expertise to help them.

Most of our stories matches up with the mental conditions of society. As a whole, people repeat the same patterns over and over again. There are only so many patterns. Nothing is new. The mental condition of your story is not new either. This is how people relate and get sucked into the story you're telling.

Remember again that a story is not a timeline. Timelines are (SNORE!) boring. It's not a chronicle of events. It's a story like you'd tell your best friend over coffee. Make it casual and conversational. Make it easy to understand.

By now you should know that you owe it to the world to share your story. It was created for that purpose. People need you. People want to hear about what you've been through and what you've learned.

If we go through things and do not share, what's the purpose of having gone through them? Sure, maybe we will individually be better people for what we've gone through, but wouldn't it be even more significant if you could impact someone else's life? You can't do that without sharing story.

Many people have pretty heart-wrenching stories. Don't compare. You may be worried that your story isn't tragic enough or that it's not that earthshattering. It is enough just as it is, right now, because it's the story that was given to you – that has brought you to this point.

One of the biggest fears for an author is to lose their reader (be boring), have them put your book down and not finish reading it. Make sure the everyday reader can understand you.

The top 5 things you can do to get your point across well:

1.     Be Clear – say what you mean and mean what you say.  Don't run off on tangents even if they seem connected.  Ask yourself if it's really relevant and if it's adding to your point.  Help the reader follow your train of thought and don't confuse them.

2.     Be Brief - most things can be cut by 50%. Don't announce what you're about to say. Don't tell them what you mean, show them without announcing it first (i.e. "I believe you're going to love this." Or "The story I'm about to share is really inspiring.") Learn to cut and enjoy cutting. Short sentences are easier to understand (this is something even I still work on every day).

3.     Be Simple – no need to use flowery language.  It doesn't actually make you sound

smarter. It just makes it harder for you to be understood. Also avoid industry jargon.  Use everyday words.

4.     Be Human – being real underlies everything!  It's crucial to keeping the reader interested, attentive and connected.

5     Show, don't tell. Think of the five senses. Describe how you feel, what you thought. For example, don't say, "I felt scared." Share your thoughts, "I felt my heart palpitating so fiercely I thought everyone could hear it and I started to sweat profusely."

Of course you don't need to sound like me or anyone else. Your writing style is who you are so write like you talk. Listen as you're writing – use your ear.

Remember, you're asking someone to go on a journey with you. When people say they like your style or the way you say things, they're really saying they like your personality. That's great!  And you don't want people to meet you after reading your book and think you aren't the same writer because you don't sound the same in person. Be yourself throughout your entire book. This is also the main reason why I don't normally recommend ghostwriting unless the ghostwriter is taking enough time with you to be able to reflect your voice.

And if you're worried that you might not be a great grammarian, check out my video about how much grammar really matters….

https://youtu.be/4pNVKqd3B5c
(bit.ly/grammardontmatter)

Throughout your book you'll have major stories and minor stories.  You might have a bigger story about your why that underlies your other stories.  And you might have some minor stories that support your teachings inside your best selling book.

## Coaching Chronicles

"My book comes out tomorrow and I'm contemplating pulling it off Amazon," Josie said as she conveyed her fears to me about her family reading her story. She was worried that they wouldn't like her sharing. She was worried other people would judge her innermost thoughts. There were some deeply private and very naked moments in there -- things she had never shared before.

I didn't need to say much. She knew. Her story mattered. It contained healing for others and she didn't write the book just to pull it at the last moment.

"What do you want, Josie?" I asked. "Do you want to stay where you are, stuck without the impact you've been craving, knowing that the people who need your help are struggling and don't know you exist yet?"

It was pretty obvious. Josie was a wounded healer – a wounded changemaker. And it cost her something to share her story.

But as soon as she released her book, a flood of appreciation flowed forward. That fueled her to become bolder and bolder and her confidence grew as the feedback came that she had shifted someone's thoughts and made an ever-lasting impact on their life.

What would've happened if she had slinked back, not shared the stories within that book? How many people would still be wandering around lost, without hope, feeling like no one understood?

Summary

There are four components to a magnetic story:

1. The Call
2. The Hole
3. The Journey
4. The Aha

There are five ways to be more interesting:

1. Be Clear
2. Be Brief
3. Be Simple
4. Be Human
5. Show, don't tell

You will have major and minor stories throughout your book.

Grab the Easy Writer workbook companion here: https://vickiegould.com/easy-writer-workbook-download/ (bit.ly/EWWorkbook)

# Step 5: Pick Your Perfect Topic, Write and Launch Your Book in 60 Days

*Whether you think you can or
you think you can't, you're right.*
*— Henry Ford*

I used to think writer's block was a real thing. I thought I had writer's block a few times even, but what I realized during my writing escapades is that writer's block is just another word for confusion ... or perfectionism, whichever you prefer.

As soon as you can get clear on what your book is about, it's much easier to break down the chapters and know what to say.

In fact, Seth Godin says there's no such thing

as writer's block because we don't encounter talker's block.

Begin by asking who you're writing the book for. Why do they need it? What do you want the reader to walk away with by the time they're done reading?

Also ask how this topic aligns with your business. Will the book allow the reader to flow into wanting your main product or service? Is it a logical piece to your prospect's journey?

Once you figure out your topic, break it down into chapters (subtopics) and further into sub-subtopics within your chapters. Laying it out this way makes it easy to complete the chapters.

And guess what? You don't even have to write the chapters in order. Write whichever comes to you and unless you have a reason why a particular sequence matters, put the most interesting chapter first.

People are tempted by the saying, "Save the best for last," to put their most intriguing chapter at the end. It's a huge mistake because if your reader has to wait to get to the good stuff, they may have stopped reading before they ever get there.

Here's a sample overview schedule for writing your Best Seller in just 60 days – we have a day by day schedule in my Easy Writer Guaranteed Amazon Best Seller Program online.  All my clients who have gone through the program (http://bit.ly/easywriterprogram ) have been able to use this to complete their book and I've heard from others who have used this on their own as well.  It works!

Day 1-10:  Get organized. Brainstorm your book ideas. Connect your idea back to the purpose of your book and what you want your reader to take action on by the time they're done reading.

Mark your 60 day finish date on your calendar. Post it on your wall.  Visualize your book finished.  Pick your book launch date. Announce your dates for accountability.

Create a list of major and minor stories you can use throughout your book.

Look up quotes you like and are applicable to the chapters and message you want to write (and save them somewhere).

This pre-writing phase is super important to the success of your book and the ease of writing in the next weeks.

Days 11 – 55:  Write at a pace of 1.5 pages a day (about 750 words).  Whether this means 1.5 pages per day for 45 days or whether it means writing more per day and taking breaks in between, you get to determine your own pace.  Structure your chapters as below:

1.      Quote
2.      Story
3.      Teachings
4.      Summary/Takeaways
5.      Call to Action

Inside your chapters, you will need to also seed your programs to turn the reader into a client. This is absolutely critical to profiting from your book.

Make sure to market your book while you're writing it so that when you're done, you'll be ready to launch it.

Day 56 - 60:  Send your book to an editor for grammar, spelling and feedback – whatever you need. Email my assistant at admin@vickiegould.com for my editor's email.

Note:  I don't recommend asking a friend to edit your book unless they're a professional editor. They don't want to hurt your feelings so might not give great feedback. But if you do decide to ask a friend or family member, be very specific on what you're looking for or you'll get, "It's great!" which is not terribly helpful.

Write out a description of your book for when you upload it to kindle.  Think of seven keywords to use and the categories (2) that would be appropriate for your book.

Get your cover back from your designer, upload your book to Amazon KDP, create your author central page and sell as many books as possible to get your book to best seller.

List your specific deadline dates.

My Launch date: _____

Number of days between launch date and now: _____

25% completion date: _____

50% completion date: _____

75% completion date: _____

100% completion date (also date to send to editor if you have one): _____

Receive back from editor date: _____

Revise book based on editor edits date:

_____

I generally have my clients write short read books. If you're counting words on a page, this chart will help you calculate how many words to aim for:

2 hours = 44-70 pages (24,000 – 30,000 words)

60 min = 33-43 pages (12,000 – 15,000 words)

45 min = 22-32 pages (9,000 – 11,250 words)

30 min = 12-21 pages (6,000 – 7,500 words)

My recommendation is to write at least 65 pages. If your book is too short, you risk it not being taken seriously.

Want to hear about how I wrote the book you're reading right now in just 4 days?

Check out the video:

https://youtu.be/jZUWdjSCKf8

Coaching Chronicles

"I've always dreamt of writing a book," Bonnie said to me. She then proceeded to tell me thirteen topics she could possibly write about. They were topics she knew something about, loved to talk about, went to school for, people asked her about and things she plain just liked.

"I have so many great ideas. I don't know which one I should go with."

She shared which one she liked the best and had even started a chapter, but when I asked how it related to her business, she said it didn't.

So I asked Bonnie what her business was, how she helped people and what her main product or service was. Then it became easy which of the topics was the one that made sense to write about that would flow right into her product or service.

Bonnie looked so excited about this clarity that she hurried off to start writing the book that she'd wanted to write for over eight years.

Summary

Pick a topic that will align with your business and flow your reader right into your product or service.

Pick a date and announce it for accountability.

Write at a rate of 1.5 pages per day for 45 days.

Upload your book to Amazon KDP, create your author central page and sell a lot of copies of your book on launch day to get to best seller.

Grab the Easy Writer workbook companion here: https://vickiegould.com/easy-writer-workbook-download/ (bit.ly/EWWorkbook)

# Jello Fluff and Extra Long Hugs

I couldn't believe what I was hearing. My husband was telling me over the phone, "He's gone." It had happened in his sleep. I heard how knotted up his voice was and I froze for a split second.

Nah, it wasn't true. My brain wasn't willing to believe it.

Just a few hours ago, my husband had called saying he couldn't get a hold of his dad. They texted every morning since mom had passed because dad lived alone. I told him he was probably out, maybe at a doctor's office where those buildings have thick walls and the reception is sometimes horrible.

My mind wanted to believe my story – that he

was just out around town like normal. He was an active 80 year old man. Sharp as a tack, always cracking a joke, and he knew everyone. He was loved by everyone.

We joked that he would go out for walks around his small neighborhood because he was canvasing for votes to be on the association board. The other place he was always at was at church. He was there two or three times a week doing the books, helping out anywhere that was needed and being a mentor to the teens.

So it couldn't be true. He was too spry. He hadn't been sick.

As I drove the hour and 15 minutes to his house to be with my husband, I ran through all the scenarios in my head of what could've happened. I cried and called my dad on the way to ask him what needed to be done first. We were in charge of the estate and trust.

What do we do now?

When I got there, the police had already come and gone. We sat and waited for the coroner and the rest was a blur. In fact, the next couple weeks were a blur as we got my husbands siblings together, cleaned and cleared out the house, set up an estate bank account, got three different stories from the probate court about what we needed, found keys for the safe deposit box and called everyone who needed to know. Plus we planned the funeral, which was just 11 days later.

I answered the questions over and over again, "What happened?" We suspected it was the heat. Dad didn't like to have to use the bathroom too often so he didn't drink on hot days and it had been a very hot week. He had been out gardening the night before.

It just didn't make sense. Could it have been

such a simple thing as drinking water? If so, I was a little mad at him for cutting our time with him short. On the other hand, I knew that God knew this was his day.

And he got what he wanted – not to be a burden to his children with illness, not to have to deal with dementia like some of his siblings had, and to be able to enjoy his every last day here on earth.

During this time, the one things I was thankful for was owning my own business. I could re-arrange my schedule and take my calls from any location. My husband took bereavement leave from his corporate job. They give a whopping three days.

I tried to be strong for my husband. I tried to concentrate on work. I tried to keep busy (something I'm actually really good at). I tried to not think too much about it or I'd cry. I pushed off some appointments but I knew I couldn't do it twice, though I wanted to. I didn't mind the work I had to do, but I didn't feel like showing up socially anywhere to put on a happy face.

The day I made jello fluff was hard for me. Dad always made it when we got together and my husband thought it would be a nice memory for when we threw my son's graduation party. It had already been scheduled and happened to be two days before the funeral. The thought of dad not ever making it again for us led me to sob and run up the stairs to cry on my husband's shoulder.

I used to think that my prior health issues with chronic Lyme Disease had made me evaluate my life enough. I had decided back then that I didn't want to live a life of regrets. From there, I had decided that I would no longer squelch who I wanted to be, that I would speak my mind more often, that I would stop putting myself last, and that I didn't want to look back ever again lamenting the life I didn't live. This was when I decided to open my business. I also decided to choose to be more happy, work on letting go of the past and not get angry, hold on to stupid stuff, or make things out to be a bigger deal than they had to be.

Dad's passing made me think even more. What was I doing with my days? How will I be remembered? What kind of impact am I making on my kids? What does it matter who I touch in the world if I don't make a big enough impact on my family?

See, dad had made a huge impact. Pastor said that the whole church was grieving because he was such a huge part of it. I heard that one of the teens he was mentoring was beside herself. There were two church members who postponed their vacations to be home for the funeral. In addition, one of the doctor's offices that I left a message for called me back to ask what happened and when the funeral was because they might want to attend.

I heard stories from all of Dad's friends about the smiling, joking, happy man who brought joy everywhere he went. They said he gave the best hugs and I knew that was true from experience. His hugs were extra long and it made you feel like he was sending extra love.

My business has never been about the money. Sure, I want fun vacations and experiences for my family, or a pair of Valentino heels … or two. Mostly though, it was about making my mark on the world, being known for something important before I died. I want to have impact and create transformation in people's lives. I want them to see in themselves what they've never seen and experience the possibilities they thought were reserved for other people. I want them to experience the life they didn't always believe they could have.

And now I'm left to wondering if that's enough for me. It's not that I want a huge funeral, but I do have to say now that I want people to say similar things they said about dad – that I was a positive influence in their lives, that I always brought sunshine with me wherever I went, and that my hugs filled them up with lots of love.

I still can't believe it's true and that he's gone. I have a new recipe that I think he would love but he'll never get to try it and I saw something at the store that made me think of him. Many days, I think of things I want to tell him or ask him but I can't.

I'm glad I didn't erase his last voicemail to me so I can replay it when I want a good laugh or just hear his voice. He had butt-dialed me and didn't know why my voicemail was talking to him, so he left a message anyway. Typical dad. I had spoken to him since then but I still wish I could call him back one more time. (2)

# Step 6:

# The Inside and the Outside

*Either write something worth reading*
*or do something worth writing.*
*- Benjamin Franklin*

While this might seem obvious, the most important parts of your book are the inside and the outside. I don't think it's given a lot of thought and they serve two distinct purposes.

**The Inside**

The inside is where you connect with your reader and upsell them into your product or service so you can create clients and income. This is how you get your return on investment.

All the juicy information and stories are inside your book. You teach, share and create connections on the inside of the book. This is where your personality shines, your vulnerability makes people relate to you and you show that you've been where your reader is and know the way out.

The inside of the book's function as a business tool is to create desire for your program so you can turn that reader into a client.

With that in mind, seeding is usually overlooked when writing a book because it's not intuitive. It's part of marketing and most writers are not trained in marketing. So even if you know what stories to include and what teaching you want to share, without seeding, it's hard to turn a reader into a client.

Seeding makes your reader aware that you have other products or services. They understand that there's more to you than just the book they're reading. Done wrong, it will feel slimy. Done right, it flows right with the book. This is why we devote a whole module in my Easy Writer online program on seeding. It's that important!

Keep in mind though that you can't say the right thing to the wrong person and you can't say the wrong thing to the right person meaning those who really adore you will be happy to hear your pitch no matter how bold. Those who aren't interested will always be offended no matter how low key you present it.

Now I want to address an idea that I've seen over and over again – writing circles. It's not a good idea.

If you're unaware of the writing circle concept, it's where a group of people who want to write a book agree to read each other's books and give feedback.

There are a number of reasons why you most likely will not get the outcome you desire from participation.

1. Everyone's in it for themselves. They will give you feedback, but it won't be of the quality you would like. Many will only skim your book – they're busy writing their own.

2. Your feedback won't be deep. Unless you're very specific about what you're looking for feedback on, you might get "I like it!" because they don't want to hurt your feelings.

3. Your circle participants are probably not your ideal client reader. An ideal client reader is the profile of your business' ideal client. If the topic is not applicable to them, how can they share appropriate feedback that you can use? It's like doing a

survey to find out a woman's favorite birthday present and polling men on where their favorite vacation spot is. The responses won't help you!

**The Outside**

The outside of the book is your book's built in marketing tool that helps convince someone to buy it. The front cover, the back cover, the description, the keywords you pick for Amazon, your price ... all of these things determine whether someone who has picked your book off the bookstore shelf (virtual or physical) is going to put it back or purchase it.

The first thing they will see is the cover and title. That's why it's important that it's eye catching, a good color, has a great title and descriptive subtitle, and invokes a particular feeling.

There are two schools of thoughts on whether

the author should be on the cover. Some feel that if you're not identifiably famous, there's no real appeal of having your photo on the front. I believe there's something to be said about being able to see someone and feel that vibe, even if they're not famous. I've done it both ways where I've been on one of my covers and not on the others.

The back cover can contain a variety of elements. It could be your author bio with photo, it could be testimonials from people who have read your book, it could be a description of your book so that a potential book buyer will want to read it. Remember if you're writing a description, it's not about you, it's about the benefits someone will experience if they read your book.

<u>Coaching Chronicles</u>

As I got on the phone with Deidre, I heard the words, "I want to write a book but best seller is no big deal. Everyone says it now. There are so many, it's diluted."

I often wonder if people who aren't best sellers say it's not a big deal because they don't think they can attain it. In the coaching world, we are well aware that people say things that are a mirror of their thoughts. Could it possibly be that they're trying to convince themselves of this idea that they don't really need nor desire it, just in case they can't have (or fail) it?

Now, it's true that there are junk books out there that hit best seller. You know why? Their marketing plan was good. The outside of their book worked for them. Maybe they sold it for zero – that's why I only teach in the Easy Writer program to launch your book to best seller in paid categories. There are definitely shortcuts that can make you feel like that best seller title you just got was less valid, which might cause you to hide instead of shine as well. Let's face it – if you're not proud of your book, you won't promote it.

Did you know that over 80% of books are sold on recommendations? If the inside of your book is lacking, it won't get talked about or referred out to friends.

Regardless if you decide best seller is something you want or not, the fact remains. While the outside can be attractive and great for getting your initial sales, you'll lack the exponential sales from people talking about your book if the inside doesn't give any value or benefits to the reader.

Summary

The two most important parts of your book are the inside and the outside. The inside is where you connect with your reader and upsell them into your product or service so you can create clients and income. The outside of the book is your book's built in marketing tool that helps convince someone to buy it. Both parts need different attention in order for your book to be successful.

Grab the Easy Writer workbook companion here: **https://vickiegould.com/easy-writer-workbook-download/** (**bit.ly/EWWorkbook**)

# Step 7:

# Fostering a Best Seller Mindset

*Most people are thinking about what they don't want, and they're wondering why it shows up over and over again.*
*-John Assaraf*

Some people think that a book is going to fix all their business problems. They lack confidence, they're unsure if they can persevere, they're not sure of their expertise and they question their value or have a hard time with the sales conversation. If your mindset is currently in the way of your business being as successful as you want it to be, a book is not going to change that. It's not a magic pill because … there ain't no such thing.

You might need to work on you.

One of the worst things that could happen after you release your book and get it to best seller is that you never mention it again, pretend like it didn't happen and don't use it in your business to get more clients. I mean, what would the purpose of writing it be if you did that?

Ask yourself why you want to write this best selling book. Is it to show people you're smart enough? Is it to prove to the world you're somebody important? If you don't already believe that you're smart enough or important enough before you write your book, you won't believe it afterwards either.

I have to admit that I assumed that some of my first clients knew what to do with their book after it hit the best seller list -- they were on a high, they were excited and celebrating. But when the celebrations ended, they stopped talking about the book. It was as if it didn't exist. They went back to the same old stale methods before their book of chasing down clients.

Why?

Now I won't go as far as to say they thought their book would sprout legs and go canvasing for clients on their behalf, but I will say that my most successful clients are using their book on a regular basis whether at book signings, speaking gigs, creating a book funnel or the like. They use it as a tool for their visibility. They've branded themselves as a best seller.

And if you're going to truly embrace the best seller status (or even just the author status), you have to be ready and willing to leverage that book for all it can do for you.

So let's put a winning mindset together for your book. Now is the time to leave behind any doubts you have about your being good enough, being famous enough, having enough followers, knowing enough, or being special enough. Now is the time to step into the glorious entrepreneur you are. This is your time to shine and be in the spotlight!

As you start to write your book, see the end goal. See the red carpet rolled out in front of you. See the clients eagerly wanting to work with you. Envision how many there will be each month. See the speaking gigs lining up. See all the things that you want for yourself and open your arms to receiving them.

Receiving is so hard for many. We "do" so we can "have" so we can "be" when, in reality, we must "be" so we can "do" and then we will "have". That's why you have to have act like a best seller before you're a best seller so you can get your best seller done!

How would a best selling author approach writing a book? How would they prioritize their writing time? What would they allow to slow them down or get in their way?

It's not supposed to be hard, though most have been taught that making money, writing a book, and being successful is hard. If it's not difficult enough, we might mistakenly think we don't deserve it. While dedication, action and commitment are necessary, making your life hard is not. Allow this process to be easy for you. Close your eyes and feel into how you want this process to work. Just ask your reader what they need to hear from you today. FEEL the ease in which the words will come to you.

During this process be committed to not operate in overwhelm or freak out mode. Think in terms of "HOW CAN I?" instead of "I can't because …." Solve whatever problems may come up for you and don't allow yourself to be stopped by any issues. This ends up being a decision.

Remember that time management is emotional management. You maintain momentum and get things done when you manage your emotions about this process. (I love the book "Loving What Is" to help turn things around)

When things come up, because they will, ask yourself, "Is this really true?", "How would my life be different if this was not true?" and "How can I turn it around?"

When you become an author and best seller, do not doubt your contribution, your genius or your right to the title. Do not down play what you've accomplished. Don't use the, "Yeah, but ....."

Consider that only .6 percent of the population

ever finishes writing and publishing their book. It's a huge accomplishment to be proud of. The title is yours because you did the work to get there. Take it.

Coaching Chronicles

"I haven't written my book yet because I'm not sure I'm cut out for this," said Nancy, "I feel like my thoughts don't come together well. People have told me in the past that I don't write well. English wasn't my best subject and I'm horrified I'll write a book that doesn't make sense."

She went on to say she didn't feel famous enough or that maybe she ought to go get some more education before she wrote the book so she'd feel more comfortable.

It sounded like everything was in Nancy's way. She even cited that she had no time because she was running a business and taking care of her family.

I asked her if all that she mentioned was really true or if fears were bubbling up now that she had decided she wanted to write her book before the end of the year.

I'd helped entrepreneurs who were labeled learning disabled in school to write best sellers. Les Brown was labeled "educable mentally retarded" and wrote a book. Could it be purely unfounded concerns keeping her back? Plenty of people like Dr. Wayne Dyer weren't famous before they wrote their book either.

So I asked her, "How badly do you want this?" She said it was the thing she thought about every day. She felt like she was being called to write this book and it should've been done years ago.

Once she confirmed this was truly what she wanted, I questioned her again, "How would a best selling author approach this?"

"They would just do it," Nancy said, "and they'd already be done."

This time though, rather than make herself feel bad for not having her book finished yet, Nancy realized she could use it as fuel to complete it.

So she sat down and mapped out her plan to write her book and picked out the date to release it. She even got on social media to declare it and ask for accountability.

She shifted to a Best Seller's Mindset.

<u>Summary</u>

Becoming a best seller is not a quick fix to any issue you have about being enough. You have to work on you.

Approach writing your book as if you are already a best seller and the right actions will follow.

Claim the title of best seller with pride because you did the work to obtain it.

Grab the Easy Writer workbook companion here: https://vickiegould.com/easy-writer-workbook-download/ (bit.ly/EWWorkbook)

# Step 8:

# Why Self-Publishing is Best

*Nothing that's worthwhile is ever easy.*
*– Nicholas Sparks, Message in a Bottle*

I cannot even begin to tell you how many of my request for discovery calls start with, "I need to get a publisher. Can you help me?" Some people are dead set on it and others think it's what they need because they don't know any better.

Some pick it because they're avoiding the technical pieces of uploading and getting their book printed. Others think that a publisher means automatic sales.

I really really wish this one was true! A

publisher actually expects you to sell your books. In fact, they'll ask you how many followers you have and how many you think you can sell in your first run of printing. They evaluate that to see if they're going to accept your pitch. You will still need to have your own marketing plan to sell your book consistently.(3)

*The following article was featured on my blog and may contain information already mentioned in this book and expands further than the self-publishing topic.*

Writing a book and getting it published used to be a huge endeavor. You had to pitch it to a literary agent who would then pitch it to a publisher and it could sometimes take years to get it accepted. These days, with kindle and the online world at everyone's fingertips, getting your book out to the world and learning how to self-publish is easier than you might think.

If you're an entrepreneur, having a book for

your business has many perks such as the added credibility, expert status and the ability to use that book to attract your ideal clients. Some even say that a book is now like a bigger, better business card.

Used correctly, your book can help you attract your tribe for years to come (so long as you continue to market it).

So first, Why self-publish?

For one, YOU KEEP ALL THE CREATIVE RIGHTS. You have the freedom to do what you want with the title, the cover and the content of your book. Why give that away?

Secondly, while it may seem enticing to use a publisher because you think they would promote your book, that's just not what happens. They don't promise to sell any copies of your book. In fact, when you pitch to them, they want to see how many people follow you on all your social media channels and they want to know how many books you think YOU'LL sell.

Lastly, self-publishing means you can get your book out faster. The exact day you're done writing, you could upload it to amazon (though I wouldn't recommend that – you might want to let it sit a couple days and do some editing …. But that's totally up to you).

My expertise is in Amazon, so let's talk about what you need to get your book uploaded and available to the world via Amazon.

Here's a "How to Self-Publish" checklist to have ready for kindle:

- Your finished ebook
- Interactive table of contents
- Cover in kindle size
- Description
- Keywords

- Title
- Subtitle
- Pricing

Once you have all those things, you can go to Amazon KDP and upload your book. You'll need an Amazon KDP account at minimum – this is where you are directly uploading your book.

Optionally, you'll want an Amazon author central page. Many new authors forget about the author central page or they plain just don't know it's available to them. The author central page allows you to share your photo, bio, your blog, your upcoming events, your videos, etc. Again, totally optional, but highly recommended if you want to be taken seriously.

(click the video below for my free, live training https://youtu.be/WUFQozFJry8 )

Now let's talk about different places you can sell your books. I want to preface this with the fact that I teach my clients to use their book as a marketing tool. The book is not the end product that they're selling. They are UPSELLING and using their book as a door-opener to new prospect and clients. Remember that you're an author-entrepreneur, right?

If you're looking for purely book sales ...

1. On your website

      – you can have a website dedicated to your book, or a page on your business website that has your book on it

2. In your shop

      –with your other info products

3. Subscribe and pay for book promotion services

      You can even look on fiverr. Please do

your due diligence on any of these services.

4.  Book signing tour

5. Amazon promotional opportunities:
Createspace (owned by Amazon) – you can select to have your book available at Barnes and Noble, along with other online retailers UPDATE: createspace will be eliminated in the near future and you can now create your print version through KDP as well.

Amazon Marketing Services (AMS) – you can create your own ads to appear in Amazon.

Amazon KDP Select – you can use this service to promote your book 5 days out of every 3 months. Please read the rules for this program because if you use it, you're obligated to be in it for 3 months and you may not sell your book anywhere else for less than what you have it listed for on Amazon.

6. Social Media
    - create a Facebook Fanpage specifically for your book

7. Facebook Groups dedicated to kindle readers

    – Just search "kindle" and you'll find a plethora of groups that promote books. Read the rules for each group to see how often, what price, when and what genre you can promote.

8. Local mom and pop book shops

9. Get creative

    – Find other ways to get the word out. Look what other authors are doing

....YouTube, contests, referrals, etc.

The main thing about selling your book is to be proactive rather than sitting around waiting for something to happen. This is a sure fire way to have nothing happen at all.

My clients are generally entrepreneurs and coaches who want a book to help those who are struggling like they once were. They are looking to create impact and change in the world, get their message out to a larger audience, and they have coaching products and packages that they promote from the 100's of dollars to the 10's of thousands of dollars that their readers will advance to purchasing. That's why they want to learn how to self-publish.

Mathematically speaking, book royalties and direct sales is a hard gig for you to make even $10k or more per month.

Most entrepreneurs who are successful with making money from their book, make it on the backend. They're happy to give their book away for free or offer it at a low cost to get that new lead in so that they can nurture and then upsell them into a bigger package that would better serve that client.

**Your book is not your end product**

To an entrepreneur, the book is not the end product. The book is the hook product. It's a lead magnet.

So with that said, the best way to sell your book so you can sell your other bigger packages, is to use a BOOK FUNNEL! Use it as opt in lead magnet. Then nurture that reader like I just said and turn him or her into a higher paying client.

THAT is the best way to be profitable with your book.

If you're eager to learn more about how to self-publish and how you can have a book that also grows your business that is not "just" a Best Seller, then I think you're going to love my Easy Writer Guaranteed Amazon Best Seller program.

It shows you and walks you through the easy step-by-step process to get your book written (with the right marketing elements inside it), shows you how to get your book to Best Seller (guaranteed) and gives you the missing piece to other book programs – it shows you how to leverage your book for clients, turning readers into paying clients in your other programs.

If that's something you'd like to do in your business, then go ahead and take advantage of this program, PLUS the awesome bonuses here:  https://vickiegould.com/amazon-group/ (4)

*The following article was featured in entrepreneur.com.*

## Two Big Book Writing Myths that Will Keep Your Book Sales Miniscule

When my first book was published, I thought it would be an overnight success based purely on the topic and the fact that I knew the world needed it. My genius marketing plan was to simply publish it. If it exists on the internet, people will find it, right?

As you can imagine, that didn't work. It's a bit like showing up to a party, not knowing anyone, trying to make a grand entrance and having zero people pay attention. In fact, it was a lot like that. Hardly anyone blinked an eye or turned their head when my book became available.

Undeterred, I decided that the ticket to my success was that coveted Amazon Best Seller ribbon. "That will solve all my problems," I thought.

My idea was that I would re-release the book, get to best seller and then it would continue to sell like hotcakes and I would just log into my sales report and see the number growing daily. That's how it works, right?

But that didn't exactly happen either. While I had successfully figured out how to get my book to best seller, after that celebratory day nothing amazing occurred.

**Myth #1: best sellers sell with ease**

All too often, I've met people who have a best-selling book, who ask me, "Now what?" The high has ended, and the book sales have dwindled off. The marketing is an afterthought because they were so focused on getting their book written.

Ideally, the best time to create a plan to sell

your book with ease is while you're writing. Set your short and long terms goals and use the numbered strategies below to help.

If you don't have a plan in place, it will feel like you're scrambling after the fact. Luckily, even if your book has been sitting idle for a while, you can pick up at any time to implement a marketing strategy.

Often I run into people who think that having a publisher will solve this problem. Either they don't know how to market their book, it seems too scary or they simply don't want to do it.

## Myth #2: a publisher will do all the marketing

These days, much is left to the author, regardless of your method of publication. If you choose to pursue a commercial publishing deal, your proposal will need to outline exactly how you will market your book.

And unfortunately, getting a publishing deal can sometime take more time than you'd like. Brendon Burchard, a well-known motivational speaker and marketing trainer and a top host on YouTube in the self-help category, had his first book, Life's Golden Ticket, rejected 15 times. Then after becoming a NY Times best-selling author multiple times over, his publisher rejected The Motivation Manifesto.

According to Derek Murphy, award-winning cover designer and owner of CreativINDIE, "Unless you're getting a deal over $100K, which means they are seriously invested in your book, you'll probably do better to self-publish."

There really is no way around having to market your book yourself. The good news is, you're the most qualified one to do it.

## The truth: how book sales are really made

It might seem a bit simple, but having an ongoing marketing campaign that you and your team will execute is critical to keeping your sales rolling in.

Think about it like this, when a new movie is coming out, like Star Wars, it is actively promoted so that the day it is released, it has the best chance at being that box office smash. But what happens as the weeks pass? Fewer people buy tickets and eventually the sales dwindle. The marketing window closes.

The same thing can happen with your book, but your window can never close. Say you're able to sell enough books to get to best seller. Afterwards, you have to keep talking about your book.

All of the ideas below with the exception of the

last two can be done before your launch date and used on an ongoing basis. Don't get overwhelmed by the sheer number of tasks to complete. This list can be done with repurposed content.

Remember, when you consistently talk about your book, you'll get consistent sales. You can do this in a number of ways.

1.    Share quotes from your book on social media and give yourself and your book title credit.

2.    Read passages from your book, leaving people with a cliffhanger so they'll want to buy it to find out the end.

3.    Offer a free chapter or a few to entice readers to want to buy the rest.

4.    Look for an author with a similar audience and suggest your book to that

audience. For example, "If you liked 'Think and Grow Rich,' you'll love [Your Book]."

5.    Create a marketing posse. This is a group of fans who are willing to share your content and give third party social proof that it's worth buying. In an article by Suw Charman Anderson, an author and journalist who is one of the UK's social media pioneers, "Only 3 percent [of book purchases] came through browsing categories. Planned search by author or topic, however, makes up a whopping 48 percent of all book choices."

6.    Make sure you're tapped into all online platforms aside from Amazon such as iBooks, Barnes and Noble, and Scribd.

7.    Take books with you everywhere you go, especially to events and networking meetings.

Many times, if you've never done something

before, it seems hard, scary or overwhelming. But once you do it, you wonder why you ever had any qualms about it.

Marketing your book is like that.  Get creative and add to the list above. Soon, you'll be automatically talking about your book everywhere you go, making sales and people will connect [Your Book] with your name. (5)

Coaching Chronicles

Over the summer of 2018 Merav Richter and her daughter Ella wrote "The Search for Maya." Merav had previously published a book with a traditional publisher and after self-publishing she told me she didn't know why anyone would ever choose a traditional publisher.

She told me that even though there were tasks she had to learn and tech she'd never done before, the high of doing it herself and watching the stats climb the day of their launch was so satisfying and exciting that she would never go back.

A lot of times we just don't know what we don't know, right? She published her other book with a traditional publisher because she thought that was the best choice at the time. She didn't know she could do it herself this easily (with some help), and be in control of all the pieces, including the launch date.

Take a listen to her feedback on the experience:
https://youtu.be/huwOIAvFqno

Summary

Self-publishing gives you many benefits such as control of your publishing timeline, contents, cover and creative rights which outweighs a traditional publisher. Plus you keep the maximum amount of royalties, even though that's not your main objective with a business book.

Getting a publisher never guarantees sales. In fact, publishers now require authors to sell them on how many books they can sell through the author's community.

Grab the Easy Writer workbook companion here: https://vickiegould.com/easy-writer-workbook-download/ (bit.ly/EWWorkbook)

# Step 9:

# Hit Publish

*The way to get started is
to quit talking and begin doing.
-Walt Disney*

Will you be ready to hit publish?

Today, right now, is the perfect time that those fallacies about your not being enough, that you can't have it all, that you have to kill yourself to get clients, play it safe, be patient, wait, be realistic, don't take risks, that what you want is too much, that you can't be a good person and wealthy, that you're too old or too young, and all the other crazy stuff that goes on your head ends.

I want you to realize and know that you can

become a superstar in your industry. You can become well-known and adored. You already are.  You just don't know it yet.

I invite you to realize the power you have inside you to have whatever you want and whatever it is that you want is fully possible, absolutely okay and nothing to be ashamed of. Today you stop making any part of you wrong for wanting a book, wanting attention, wanting the spotlight or feeling "extra."

Because writing your book is more than just writing a book. It's like your coming out party. It's where you share the truth of who you are, unapologetically so that you can help others who struggle like you once did. It's when you step up to the calling on your life and stop ignoring the nudge to write your book and finally do it.

Imagine your ideal client reading your book. How much will it help them?  Visualize who that person is. What are their qualities? Where are they struggling? What are they crying about at night? What are they hiding from their friends and family? In what ways can you give them hope?

Once you're done writing your book, the moment of truth arrives and stares you in the face in the form of a yellow button that asks you if you're ready to publish your book. How will you answer?

Remember the statistic of the .6 percent that actually hit publish? For every 1000 people who want to write a book, 30 people finish and 6 hit publish. That means that 24 people finish and are too scared to put it out into the public.

When I talk to people about their book, it's never a question about the journey or story they have to share. That's always impactful. It's never a question about their skill set either. They know exactly how to help people. But something happens when it comes time to write the book. That's why people don't start. And that's why people don't hit publish. It's the same thing. FEAR.

Maybe your fear comes from not knowing what to expect or not knowing what to do. That's probably why you're reading this book – to get advice and steps from someone who's done it multiple times before. When you know what's coming or that you have someone to hold your hand, it's not so scary, right? People have said that my Easy Writer program is like that because I put in step-by-step videos too. It is like someone holding your hand, sharing step by step how to pick the best topic, align it with your business, write, publish and launch your book to best seller, then answer the, "Now what?" question in depth so you can not just share your experiences and expertise, but also profit from your book.

Plus, I don't let you slink away in the corner and chicken out from hitting publish.

Now there's one thing you absolutely cannot avoid when you put out a book – opinions. Everyone has an opinion from the color of your cover to the text and the photo you might include of yourself, not to mention your thoughts expressed inside the book. I won't say it doesn't hurt a bit because it does, but remember that sometimes people's feedback is a reflection of what's going on for them. Ask yourself if the feedback is valid where you can truly improve or if it's not applicable and let it go.

Do not let one person's negative comment (or even online public review) of your book dim your light or weaken your zest for what you do. Your purpose and calling is never modified by what someone else says.

I love affirmations to help create positivity in

my life and what I've learned is that if I don't believe, or have any doubts about what I'm affirming, it doesn't matter how many times I say it.

For example if you don't believe you're a good writer, saying it over and over again in the morning in the mirror won't make you believe it all of the sudden.

Work up to it with affirmations like these:

I am working on becoming a good writer.
I can become a good writer.
I choose to learn to become a good writer.
I have the capability to be a good writer.
I love writing more and more each day.
I create opportunities where I can shine with my writing.
I am allowed to be a great writer.
I am a writer.
I am a good writer.
I am a great writer.

What other affirmations could help you become more confident to hit publish as you're writing or when you're done with your book?

Coaching Chronicles

We had set the date and planned to upload her book to Amazon's KDP platform when Melody said, "I'll do it tomorrow." She proceeded to tell me all the things that she needed to do and avoided uploading the book for another day and a half.

I was worried it wasn't going to be listed on Amazon in time for her launch date but she was acting cool as a cucumber and I couldn't quite figure out why. I was starting to wonder if she was hoping it wouldn't be there. Luckily she did finally upload it and her book was accessible right before she needed to announce to her community that it was available to buy.

Then she stalled again. The morning came and she hadn't posted a single thing on social media and had not sent out an email to her list.

I called her on the phone and asked what was happening. "You're going to miss the date you told everyone it would be out. They won't even know about it. What is going on?"

"I'm scared," she said, "What if it doesn't make sense to anyone? What if it was a waste of my time? What if the whole thing was a mistake?"

I reminded her that we had talked about this before in our coaching calls – that it is scary to put yourself out there, all raw for everyone to see, but the whole purpose of sharing the stories was bigger than she was. It was about the other people. How much did she want to help them?

Together, we took some deep breathes, visualized the success of that day, remembering the reason for her calling.

In her last long deep breath, she said, "Okay, I'm ready. Freak-out averted. Let's do this!"

She announced the availability of her book to her community through her social media platforms around noon, personally reaching out by phone and text, and emailed everyone who had asked for a reminder from her previous marketing campaign.

And it all ended well. By evening, she hit the best seller list and went on to get on stages and do book signings internationally.

## Summary

Having fears when publishing your book is normal but in order to serve the world and help those who are struggling, you have to be willing to consider them more than your comfort level.

Now is the time to decide that you're enough as you are – you don't need to be more famous, have more followers, get more education, or live more life. You and your experience up until this moment are enough.

Waiting to publish your book only leaves the exact people who need you most to continue to wait as well. If you knew there was a solution to your problems that someone was holding back from you, how would you feel? That's why now is the time to begin and finish your writing journey.

Grab the Easy Writer workbook companion here: https://vickiegould.com/easy-writer-workbook-download/ (bit.ly/EWWorkbook)

# Step 10:

# Figuring Out -- Now What?

*The only limits for tomorrow are the doubts
we have today.*
*–Pittacus Lore, The Power of Six*

This is the chapter that I'm most excited to share because so many people end their writing journey at a published book. This is also why I feel I'm different from other book coaches. I know it's critical to answer the question, "Now what?"

Knowing that you have major stories and minor stories where your main story shares your why, you can used these to create what I call "storywheels" for your business.

Your storywheel is how you can spider out your story and repurpose content on multiple platforms. You can pitch all sorts of media with topics and stories plucked right out of your book.

In the center of your circle is one of your stories. Let's take your why story as an example – this is the story about why you do what you do and what led you there. When you pitch, you can add some teaching tips if it's pertinent.

When you are able to create content for all those platforms, your followers will start to say, "You're everywhere!" What they haven't figured out is that you're re-using content from your book!

Do you see now that with your book, you are creating never-ending content? Most people need to hear the same thing from you 10 or even 20 times. The world is full of short attention spans so don't feel shy to re-use the topics and stories in your book. You can probably say the same thing in multiple ways pretty easily because you were the one who wrote it in the first place.

In the process, you create what I call the "Omnipresence Circle." Starting with your book, you use your story and content that you can then create a livestream for, reuse for teaching in a telesummit, then share in a podcast …. and on and on until it comes full circle.

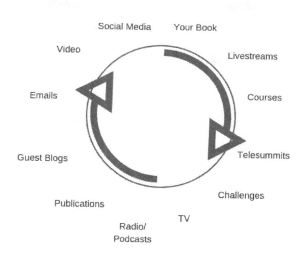

Do not forget from Step 2 that creating a book funnel is an important step to leveraging your book. This is the piece that helps your book grow legs and work for you. An automated funnel will allow you to develop your business with consistent clients and wake up to messages in your inbox from people who want to work with you further.

I remember a trip I took to Maui for almost 2

weeks. I wanted to make sure I wasn't tied to my computer or my phone so I set my social media content to post automatically and I ran an ad for my funnel. While it's not required to run ads (you can promote organically too, it just takes longer to grow your list), it helped me to come home to 7 appointments to my inbox -- a full schedule of discovery calls when I returned.

Many entrepreneurs have told me that they feel like they have to work while on vacation or at a conference because if they don't, they won't have anything in the pipeline when they return. Creating a funnel creates time freedom for you while helping you have consistent monthly income.

Coaching Chronicles

"I want it all," Dee Dee said. "I want the book, the speaking gigs, my course done, my followers growing on social media and more.

Then I want to get corporations to hire me to come in and help their leadership staff."

And I told her of course she could have it and what it entailed was a strategy. The book would share her expertise, she could do videos online to grow her following and we'd put together a plan to have a book funnel.

"You must be willing to talk about your book everywhere and on every platform. You cannot be shy. Your book title will become equivalent to your name," I told her. She said she was in.

About a month after her book hit best seller, a local magazine featured her success. Then TV noticed the feature and asked her to be on the following day. Since then, she's been on TV again sharing her story and her book.

She's currently working on a course, going deeper than her book so that she can take the book as a companion to the course into corporations to help them with their staff.

## Summary

Your book writing journey can't end when it's published. Leveraging your story and your book is the most important strategy to have in place after you've launched to best seller so that your book can help grow your business.

Getting seen on various media will help spread your message, create more impact, grow your community and create more clients for your business, but you must be willing to put in the work and be consistent with it.

Grab the Easy Writer workbook companion here: https://vickiegould.com/easy-writer-workbook-download/ (bit.ly/EWWorkbook)

# Conclusion

*How wonderful it is that nobody
need wait a single moment before
starting to improve the world.*
*- Diary of Anne Frank*

If you've been taking non-encouraging book writing advice from people who haven't written their book, stop.

If you've been feeling called to write your book, start!

Writing a book and publishing it to best seller will change your life. I've mentioned some of this before and it's worth mentioning again – my clients have become #1 international best selling authors.  They've been able to land Tedx talks, get on TV, share their expertise on multiple stages, be asked on telesummits, been given opportunities for book signings, published articles in well-known publications, been guests on podcasts and radio, improved their businesses, closed $2M deals, gained more recognition, won awards -- I could go on and on. And some of them have even written multiple books!

What's the secret to their success? Leveraging that best selling book and finding the confidence to show up fully, ask for what they want and go for it. They mention and use their book everywhere. People know they have written a best seller. They fostered that best seller mindset and set out into the world to make waves of positive change.

So.....

Write something that's meaningful to you. Write something you'd be proud to leave behind. Write something that shares your story. Write something that makes you feel good.

And write it NOW.

If you need help, I'm here with programs to fit whatever stage of business you're in. The two main programs I'd recommend are the Easy Writer Guaranteed Amazon Best Seller Program and my one-on-one coaching package. You can find both (and more) on my website at www.vickiegould.com/coaching/. I'd be happy to help you decide which program is right for you. Just write me at vickie@vickiegould.com.

In the meantime, I'd like share the experiences of my past clients. It's my hope that you'll see some of yourself in these three clients and that you see what is possible for you too.

Name: Shaneil Stewart

Enrolled Program: Easy Writer Guaranteed Amazon Best Seller

Shaneil and I had known each other for about a year and a half. We had met at a coaching conference and stayed in contact. So when she told me that she had been wanting to write a book, I was surprised. She had never mentioned it before.

Shaneil had felt a nudge in the fall of 2016 that she was being called to share her story but she had told herself she wasn't ready. She needed to become more famous first. Comparing herself to Tony Robbins and Oprah, she felt she needed to be more like them in order for her book to be successful.

She told me she had thought about a book years ago, but never let it stay in her mind long. She had pushed it aside for, "later." Sometimes it's frightening to say such a thing out loud.

But once she admitted it, she started to question herself. Was it the right time? Maybe she should wait. Again, that famous thing came up. Did she have the time with all the other things going on in her life and business? How in the world was she going to pull this off? It seemed so huge and daunting to try to write and publish it.

She didn't know how to structure the book. She wasn't sure what to say inside. She didn't know how to organize everything so that it flowed and made sense. She knew she wanted to share her story, but she was afraid it wouldn't be interesting enough. And what about the topic? Which of the four potential topics in her head was the right one?

All she knew was that this book was tugging at her heart and that she wanted to help people.

As soon as she committed that writing her book was a true desire of hers, she enrolled in my program so she could get step-by-step guidance. Within 12 weeks, she had her book written with everything she needed to go with it, launched to best seller.

Afterwards, she told me that it was by far the scariest thing she's ever done. So many uncertainties came up for her along the way, but because we had set a pace to finish within those 12 weeks, she didn't have the opportunity to set her book aside and let the fears take a hold of her.

Now she uses her book in a funnel that allows her to get clients on autopilot. She implemented a series of emails to go with it and upsells those clients into her one-on-one package that she's since doubled at least twice.

Listen to Shaneil share her experience here: https://vickiegould.com/shaneil-easy-writer-interview/

Name: Andrew (Andy) Smith
Enrolled Program: Easy Writer Guaranteed Amazon Best Seller Program

Andy had been trying to write his book for the last 10 years. He had picked it up, put it down, picked it up, put it down over and over again over the course of those years and he was frustrated.

He thought, "It's so true that writing a book is long and hard. It's virtually impossible. I'm never going to get this thing done. I might as well scrap the whole thing and give up."

Thing was, it was a big desire of his to have a book. Part of it was for him – to say he had done it. And part of it was that he felt he really had something worthwhile to contribute to the world with this book.

He just couldn't get it out of his head.

The words would come sometimes, but almost never when he willed them to. He'd get bits and pieces of things he thought he should put into it as he was driving down the road or taking a shower. It seemed like at the most inopportune times, a great idea would come to him. Some of them he'd forget before he had a chance to write them down.

Eventually it seemed like his book was in bits and pieces. There were pieces in his journal, half-thoughts on slips of paper, parts in the notes on his phone and little reminders on sticky notes.

It just wasn't coming together.

Do you want to know why? Andy had never considered what he wanted for the book. All he knew was that he wanted to have a book.

It wasn't until he got into the book prep section of my program that he finally answered the questions of: Who is this book for? What do you want them to walk away with?  What's the purpose of the book for you? What action do you want the reader to take when they're done?

Once he got clear, all of the sudden he had something to aim towards. He could reverse engineer exactly what the book would help people with and what topics and subtopics were most appropriate for it.

In a matter of the 12 weeks, Andy accomplished what he had not been able to accomplish for the last 10 years. His book launched it to best seller April of 2017.

Since then, Andy has been much clearer in his business as well. He knows exactly what programs he wants to offer and who they're for.

Hear Andy's experience here:

https://vickiegould.com/andy-easy-writer-interview/

Name: Karen Donaldson

Enrolled Program: One-on-One Book Coaching and 90 Minute Book Coaching Intensive

Karen was part of the statistic that had written her book but left it on her computer. She actually had two books hidden there for over 4 years and when she came to me she said she hadn't published them because she didn't know what to do with them. However, she felt the books were valuable to her business and could be helpful to her future clients.

So we created a strategy to revisit the books, make sure they aligned with her business mission and launch them to best seller.

She asked, "Which book should I launch first?" and I shocked her by saying, "Why not both at the same time?" Her marketing could do double duty and we wouldn't need to space out the release of each book with two separate campaigns. It had never occurred to her that this was an option.

I continued to shock her when we discussed the release date and I asked her why it couldn't be in two weeks. We had finished the revisit of the book and it was ready. Why wait?

At first Karen said she wasn't ready. She shrieked and gulped on the phone. But in the end, when she could find no reason not to release the books in two weeks, she was excited to see her vision of these books become a reality.

Two weeks later, after executing the best seller launch strategy, Karen became a double best selling author, internationally.

Karen uses her books in her client marketing and for her speaking gigs, especially corporate ones. She gives a copy to the conference coordinator to help push them over the edge to say yes to booking her and she also gives a copy to the audience.

She's gotten additional one-on-one and group clients from the audience. That means she's getting paid to speak at the company and then getting paid again from the participants who want additional coaching! Karen's last estimate was that her initial books have brought in nearly 6 figures of additional business for her.

Epilogue: Karen recently released her third book, two years after her double best sellers. It's now the second book in a series after one of the firsts. She launched to best seller internationally again this time and she stayed at #1 for over seven days.

Check out Karen's latest book and what she's up to here:

https://www.instagram.com/therealkarendonaldson/

# About the Author

Vickie Gould is known as The Words Lady™ and is a 9-time best selling author with books like *Hit Publish!* and *Standing in the Gap*. She's helped nearly 100 others become best sellers who are able to share their stories more impactfully all around the world, grow their reach and gain more clientele.

Vickie is a certified Law of Attraction Practitioner through Joe Vitale, certified Divine Living coach through Gina Devee, and a Global Leader in Lisa Nichols' programs where she was asked to be a master speaker facilitator helping to teach storytelling, evaluate participants and offer personalized feedback.

She was nominated for the SEEN Magazine Changemaker award for 2018 and named #44 of the top 100 in Saving Her Elegance (SHE) "100 Women You Should Know" Campaign.

Vickie believes that stories are the ultimate connector and the most critical piece of business to be able to share. She believes that books are the way that we can live forever in our words and create a long lasting legacy. Just about everyone has a book inside of them.

She's often quoted saying, "The most transformational book you read is the one you write."

You can find her at www.vickiegould.com
Email her at vickie@vickiegould.com

Facebook FanPage:
www.facebook.com/vickiegouldcoach

Facebook Group:
www.facebook.com/groups/vickiegouldcoaching

Instagram @vickiegould
https://www.instagram.com/vickiegould/

Twitter @vickie_gould
https://twitter.com/vickie_gould

Linkedin @vickiegould
https://www.linkedin.com/in/vickiegould/

Pinterest@vickiegouldcoach
https://www.pinterest.com/vickiegouldcoach/

# References

(1) Gould, Vickie. "The Difference Between an Author-Author and an Author-Entrepreneur and Why You Need to Know" Writer's Digest, 30 Aug. 2018, http://www.writersdigest.com/editor-blogs/questions-and-quandaries/business/the-difference-between-an-author-author-and-an-author-entrepreneur-and-why-you-need-to-know Accessed 21 Oct 2018.

(2) Gould, Vickie. (2018) *Courageous World Catalysts II.* Seattle, Washington: Amazon Digital Services LLC

(3) Gould, Vickie. "10 Big Lies You've Been Told about Writing and Selling Your Business Book" Vickie Gould Blog, 10 Oct. 2017. https://vickiegould.com/blog/business-strategy/10-big-lies-youve-been-told-about-writing-and-selling-your-business-book/ Accessed 21 Oct 2018.

(4) Gould, Vickie. "A Beginners Guide to Self-Publishing (and Other Avenues to Sell Your Books)" Vickie Gould Blog, 17 Nov 2017. https://vickiegould.com/blog/book-marketing/a-beginners-guide-to-self-publishing-and-other-avenues-to-sell-your-books/ Accessed 21 Oct 2018

(5) Gould, Vickie. "2 Big Book Writing Myths That Will Keep You From Achieving Big Profits" Entrepreneur.com, 24 Jul. 2018, https://www.entrepreneur.com/article/316870 Accessed 23 Oct 2018.

54881412R00107

Made in the USA
Columbia, SC
09 April 2019